Also by Graham Roumieu

Me Write Book

Mike Randolph

This is Graham Roumieu's fourth
or fifth book. He is willing to
accept honorary doctorates from
any reputable learning institution.
Learn more about Graham at
WWW.ROUMIEU.COM

BIGFOOT

I NOT DEAD

GRAHAM ROUMIEU

A PLUME BOOK

PLUME
Published by the Penguin Group
Penguin Group (USA) Inc., 375 Hudson Street, New York, New York 10014, U.S.A.
Penguin Group (Canada), 90 Eglinton Avenue East, Suite 700, Toronto,
Ontario, Canada M4P 2Y3 (a division of Pearson Penguin Canada Inc.)
Penguin Books Ltd., 80 Strand, London WC2R 0RL, England
Penguin Ireland, 25 St. Stephen's Green, Dublin 2, Ireland
(a division of Penguin Books Ltd.)
Penguin Group (Australia), 250 Camberwell Road, Camberwell,
Victoria 3124, Australia (a division of Pearson Australia Group Pty. Ltd.)
Penguin Books India Pvt. Ltd., 11 Community Centre, Panchsheel Park,
New Delhi – 110 017, India
Penguin Group (NZ), 67 Apollo Drive, Rosedale, North Shore 0632, New Zealand
(a division of Pearson New Zealand Ltd.)
Penguin Books (South Africa) (Pty.) Ltd., 24 Sturdee Avenue, Rosebank,
Johannesburg 2196, South Africa

Penguin Books Ltd., Registered Offices: 80 Strand, London WC2R 0RL, England

First published by Plume, a member of Penguin Group (USA) Inc.

First Printing, May 2008
10 9 8 7 6 5 4

Copyright © Graham Roumieu, 2008
All rights reserved

Art photographed by Eden Robbins.

 REGISTERED TRADEMARK—MARCA REGISTRADA

CIP data is available.

ISBN 978-0-452-28956-7

Printed in Mexico

BOOKS ARE AVAILABLE AT QUANTITY DISCOUNTS WHEN USED TO PROMOTE PRODUCTS OR SERVICES.
FOR INFORMATION PLEASE WRITE TO PREMIUM MARKETING DIVISION, PENGUIN GROUP (USA) INC.,
375 HUDSON STREET, NEW YORK, NEW YORK 10014.

BIGFOOT

I NOT DEAD

Dear People,

May have notice Bigfoot not around much last couple of years. All start with tragic hot plate related fire at Bigfoot compound... So scare by fire and sad about burn ravioli that Bigfoot just run. Eventually run so far decide no point going back. Some people think I perish in flames, others say I stage death. Neither true. Instead, like Kerouac Bigfoot deci to travel land. Like Odysseus have hard time get back, romance some ladies and slay monster both figurative and real. Like OJ, just want run down highway for little while and clear name later. Most important thing be that Bigfoot want share experiences and what they teach about life, love, self. So peace on Earth can finally be acheive.

Love,

Bigfoot

SAD TIMES

Bigfoot get real down sometimes.
Hard not to.
Bigfoot give best of self to world
and still get treat
like shit.

Wonder what point in trying?
Why Bigfoot go on?
Then I remember.
It totally crystal-clear.
Me totally look
awesome on camera.

This Just In

WHAT YOU NEED KNOW ON THE STREET

SELF IMPROVE

Bigfoot got get more perfect.
Refine Bigfootocity. Pull together.
Think outside box. Lose ten pound.
Learn speak the French. Ballroom dance.
Demonstrate superior knowledge of
fine wine at dinner party in charming
non-pretentious manner.
Be Oscar Wilde of woods,
It so hard.
Brain size of apricot. So, so hard
think good.
Maybe if eat Kelsey Grammer
of Frasier fame, will absorb
him soul and all attribute
like McDonald's combo meal.

WATERSHIT DOWN

Went back to old neighborhood a while
ago. Think it maybe nice get back to
roots, breathe in fresh country air.
Get there and was very surprise.

Toad stools all cover in graffiti.
Burbling brook all full of needle
and barf and fuzzy bloated corpses.
Squirrels now bury rock of crack instead
of nuts.
Homeless bee everywhere.
Feel sorry for my old friends.
Then some asshole squish blueberry
on hood of Bigfoot limo.
Think learn them lesson.
Buy up whole block for cheap and
have bulldoze for condo developmen

Blind Date

LOOK BOTH WAY

How many reflective vest Bigfoot
have to wear before people **stop**
run Bigfoot over on foggy mountain
road at night?! One or two time
a year maybe understandable, but
    one or two time a week? Have
vest and blinky light and road flare
and everything but still wind up
getting cut down like stalk of wheat.
Maybe if soccer mom everywhere
lay off wine spritzer and stop talk
on cell phone while drive Escalade
maybe **this not** happen. Maybe if you
not act like my fault maybe I not
throw you kids off cliff.

MANNERS

CLARIFICATION

Should no have explain this again but seem you people just not get it throug you thick skulls.
BIGFOOT NOT GRANT WISHES LIKE LEPRECHAUN OR GENIE. Only exception be that if you want wish for kick in you face then go ahead and rub me belly. Otherwise, fuck off and get job.

FAN LETTER

Q Bigfoot, you come be in school play? We no can pay but everybody here love and admire Bigfoot. Love, Tommy J. AGE 8, Newark, N. J. ●

A You know Timmy, world not some magic place where can write letter to famous important person like Bigfoot and get something for nothing because you a kid. You probably not have daddy so not know right from wrong. You trying to steal from Bigfoot. Maybe tomorrow you murder old lady for $5. You scum of earth Tammy.

Q Bigfoot, when my Guinea pig wake up? Parents say he sleeping in box in ground in back garden. Suzie, Age 9, Toronto, Canada

A Actually Suzie Guinea pig dead and Bigfoot already dig up and eat. If want back Bigfoot probably poop out bones and fur in day or so. Very delicious, raise him right, he taste like love.

MAJESTY

It true Bigfoot royalty. King of forest.
Not one for formality though. More
ceremonial figurehead.
Like keep casual, approachable,
    but insolence not tolerated.
Have big parade for assert power.
Big pomp and spectacle and balloon.

Biggest perk of be king is get drink first at watering hole. It good because Bigfoot really hate commoner backwash.

Nature Boy

Watching nature shows on
 T.V. usually make Bigfoot sick.
Full of mistake and boring.
T.V. show mans come in MY woods,
act like they own the place, whisper
dumb stuff, trample Bigfoot berry bushes,
shoot tranquilizer dart around all
 willy-nilly and keep Bigfoot
awake with bright light and
stupid cellphone ring tone.
All for nothing too!
Shows total crap. They have
 no idea what talking about.

If really want to know, why not
they just come ask Bigfoot?
Got all sort of juicy shit on
every animal.

BIGFOOT GUIDE FOR EVERYTHING EVER WANT KNOW ABOUT FOREST ANIMAL

DANNY - Eastern Gray Squirrel
- FUCKWIT

LEROY - Grizzly Bear
- I hear he totally impotent

M.C. HAMMER - Woodpecker
- Is a sucker M.C.

BERNARD - Beaver
- Al Qaeda sleeper agent

MR. MIGGINS - Some kind of weasel
- Pervert

VICTORIA - Butterfly
- Tax cheat

PLANS

Is beautiful day. Maybe Bigfoot
go for walk. Maybe go eat the
chickens. Go lay by stream and
practice yelling.   Be nice.
No, wait, can't. What if girl call
that Bigfoot meet at bar last night?
She hot.
Pretty sure she say she vegan.
I say I vegan too to make her like.
No chickens for Bigfoot,
Bigfoot no have cell phone so no go anywhere.
Fuckme hate today.

I NOT BRAGGING, BUT...

You may have hear already. I not surprise
if you did. Sort of big deal really,
After years of plan and blood and sweat
and tear, Bigfoot dream finally realize.
Going be off-off-off Broadway
musical base on Bigfoot life.
Some kinks still need straighten out
but basically go like this:

① All dark, then flute and drum go DOO-DOO-DOO-TEEE-DO

② Bigfoot come on stage and sing song
about Bigfoot life.

③ Lots of dance and pretty lady.

④ Blinking light.

⑤ More dance and sing

⑥ All dark, then flute and drum go DO-DEE-DOOT-TO-EEEE

⑦ Some applauses

SCHOOL HARD KNOCKS

Because Bigfoot so big and strong and handsome, every time go out jerks try pick fight with me. Think they big and tough and think Bigfoot thing to conquer like mechanical bull. Say things that not nice. Say stuff like "██████. I going get medieval on you ass Bigfoot!" Bigfoot still live slightly ███ stone age existence so not much of threat. Give them pre history lesson.

DIRECTION

Might as well come clean.
Bigfoot not as confident as might
first seem. For example get lost often.
Most of time not know where am.
People think Bigfoot master of woodland
navigation. Move through darkness
like velvet torpedo.
Not true. Mostly just
    Stumbling around smashing
head into branches trying recognize
where am but every fucking tree
look the same. For love of God, next
time you go camping and hear me
screaming in distance don't run
away COME HELP BIGFOOT.

INJUSTICE

Police,
Stop trying arrest Bigfoot for vagrancy. How many times I have explain? I pee over there, over there and over there. Technically make it Bigfoot territory. You see broken stick and piece of ~~beer~~ fry chicken over there? That kitchen, you standing in foyer. Get out of Bigfoot house if you no have warrant.

SLIP-SLIDE AWAY

Bigfoot wonder how life be different if never decide leave woods all those year ago, Consider what could have be. Never meet any of you, no have adventure, but also never have hurts and hard time. Bigfoot bite forbidden apple and no could turn back.

Deep pool in cold mountain stream turn into hot tub with barf and wig float in it, echo of canyon now microphone feed back, water now Zima. It occur to Bigfoot maybe the never anything worth try escape ~~far~~ from.

Neighbor

Lot of people make all big deal about bears. I say it not bears have worry about, it goddamn wolverines. Those bastard <u>crazy</u>.

One move in across street and like I no can leave house anymore. Wolverine always sit on stoop and drink beer and stare. Creepy. Always play loud music late at night and burn garbage on lawn and rev motorcycle. Hate so much but Bigfoot no can do anything because I chicken shit.

Hear wolverines can spit acid and bench press like 500 pounds.

DEAR LADY

Hello. Bigfoot have been watching you.
You get present Bigfoot leave on
you lawn? Make self, come from heart.
Hope you like. Take long time to
get just right. Express feeling good.

You not come out of house lately,
Understand maybe you want take it slow.
Have take time to think perhaps,
No rush. Bigfoot cool like that.
Like lady who play hard to get.

BIG GREENIE

Everybody all uppity about environment and global warm. Bigfoot have warn you for years but no one listen. Al Gore get Nobel Prize, Bigfoot get tasered in shower at mental hospital. Wake up in Cuba wearing orange jump suit and bag over head.

Hot weather all of time make Bigfoot shed like crazy. If you find hair in you food or drink it probably mine. 10% chance it Bigfoot pube. That taste hard get out of mouth.

Frankly if eat one probably just better if kill self.

GOOD TIP FOR HELP SAVE ENVIRONMENT

- Lower carbon emission by chase Bigfoot on floating log in river rather than truck, helicopter or hovercrafts. Promise I run slower if do so.

- Roll up dead sweat skin behind ear and enjoy as delicious cheese substitute. My ear make havarti. What ear cheese you be?

- Turn off exterior light on house. Save electricity and make easy for Bigfoot punch yappy dog in face.

FIT

Used to be that Bigfoot hate being
chased around by angry villagers.
Worst when they show up on
Sunday morning when I be out partying
night before. No fun fight for
life when have bad hangover.
Really piss Bigfoot off.
Then after few months notice run
not so bad. Sort of enjoy.
Notice have more energy during
week. Slim down lots.
Ask villagers if they not mind increase
chase from 10 mile to full 26 mile
marathon.
Now have sponsorship deal with shoe
company. Be on cover of Sports Illustrated.
Angry Villager Chase going to be
demonstration sport in next olympics.

STEAL FROM RICH, POOR.

Sick of shitty forest food,
Sick of watch all forest friend starve
because all have eat is spider and mosses.
Bigfoot start take food from campground.
Many camper think cute, do right thing and
not resist. Others make troubles.
Park warden get pissy,
He label Bigfoot an outlaw,
Put bounty on head.
Admit Bigfoot might cross line when
move from steal food to cash, car, jewel
and identity theft.

In hindsight Bigfoot no should have
shit where eat.

POEMS

Smile Laugh Cry

Smile is pretty lady who say "hello".
Laugh is fart like whistle - "WOOO!"
Cry is lady slap for whistle fart "WOOO!".
Smile is balloon in hand.
Laugh is balloon with funny clown face.
Cry is balloon from clown funeral who die in fire.
Smile is pizza lunch.
Laugh is soda bubble tickle nose.
Cry is eat at clown funeral who die in fire.

HOT DOGS

How Bigfoot love
Organ meal in tube
Tell me, that testes I taste?
Dinner bell a-ringin'
Oh no can get enough
Good eatz!
Spicy face meatz!

THE QUESTION

Bigfoot known for have big feet.
Please stop ask if have big genital.
Joke stop be funny long time ago.
Why you people still laugh at tired, childish crap?
Don't treat Bigfoot like clown.
Hold press conference on Bigfoot fact
finding mission to Darfur civil conflict
and resulting horrific refugee crisis that
it have spawned.

Trying shed light on and open dialogue about what potentially be worst humanitarian crisis of 21st century and all you journalist giggle and make dick joke. Throw me peanuts and try get me pose for picture with you kids like I some dumbfuck zoo bear or ~~George~~ George Clooney

MATE

What Bigfoot want in special lady is for be nice to Bigfoot. Tell story, sing song, comb Bigfoot hair and say "Shhh... it OK.". Maybe also say dirty thing. Like lady with clean credit record and filthy mouth.

Tell me you fart in me hand and I yours forever, sexy.

Also need be tolerant
of Bigfoot lifestyle.
Sometimes gone for months at time,
come home drunk and have tranquilizer
dart in neck. Maybe lipstick on neck fur.
Smell like lady perfume.
Not what it look like.
No get angry
Just important science experiment
Bigfoot sometime participate in.

Take me breath away.

GOOD HELP HARD FIND

Bigfoot hold tryouts for ~~his~~ sidekick.
Make take simple test to see if
qualified for job. Get sense school
System not emphasize fundamentals
enough anymore.

TEACH YOU CHILDREN WELL

Advice to all aspiring mythological creature out there: no give it away for free. You talented and essential to society so you services have money value. If see documentary film crew shooting you and say something like "sign this standard contract" or "this be good exposure for you!", run away. They might seem nice. Might give free muffin or gum but whole time they just want screw you. They no pay you, They take pure artistic vision and floss greedy filthy corporate ass with it. Take you baby and throw it in dumpster of clam chowder and battery acid.

Also, if go to casting call and producer close door and ask you take off clothes, that not normal. Yes, me know everybody see video of young Bigfoot shaking junk on internet.
Highly erotic? Yes. Right? No.
Learn from Bigfoot folly.

PUNKS

Hate teenager, treat Bigfoot with no respect. Get out of here with you rap music and bad moustache. Get off my lawn. GET OFF LAWN OR I CALL COPS! What you call me you little shit? It you who smash Bigfoot antique bird bath don't think me not know.

HUNT

You probably not believe if I tell you.
Maybe that for best.
Swear Bigfoot tell truth.
Many year ago Bigfoot
get recruit as secret agent,
Perfect candidate. No friend,
no family, hard capture on film, kill good,
eat what kill, can-do attitude. Fun like big
game at first. Then thing get serious.
Get send into wooded area for stop
animal revolution against peoples.
Infiltrate and destroy. Bigfoot hands
stain in blood of fellow forest
creature. Pop heads like sheet
of bubble wrap. Still haunt me.
When all done agency deny knowledge
of Bigfoot. Dump me in gutter.
Now you read this you phone be tapped.

HATERS

Bigfoot have a lot of critic. People go around and gossip bad about me. Say I a thug, that I evil to core, that I crass, perverted monster. Really they just jealous, Bigfoot live free, do whatever want.

If Bigfoot want pay thousands dollars an hour to huck

hot dog at beautiful women in unicorn costume who has right to stop Bigfoot? Maybe me did sell out, become too materialistic, but if you ain't dancing in unicorn costume or handing Bigfoot hot dogs, get the hell out of me face.

I BE YOU EVERYTHING

Do you suck? Get Bigfoot as spirit guide animal and suck no more. Listen: eagle stuck up, wolf a nut licker, bear a drunk. Bigfoot only good choice. A^{++}. Spirit Animal Monthly describe Bigfoot: "...a delight. He pushes a role normally mired in tradition in new and exciting directions. Also good at parties. Black tie, kegger, funeral, bris, whatever. Also good for kill you enemy. Me rates reasonable. Get complimentary pen.

grenade

GOOD OLD DAY

Woods used be about
survival of fittest. Kill or be kill,
Best days of Bigfoot life. Smash all day,
sleep like baby at night.
Now everybody go all soft,
Violence not "cool".
Now all about compassion
and reason and understanding.

Used to be Bigfoot smash
hiker with rock and later
that night share smash anecdote on Carson.
Now everybody hold candlelight
vigil for hiker and newspaper
call me vulgar out dated animal
and people say awful thing about me
on internet. It hurt Bigfoot feeling,
make cry, want kill all of you.

YOU CRY TOO IF HAPPEN TO YOU

It me birthday and nobody come.
I so very sad.
Just me and cake and hat and tears.
Maybe think secret surprise party happen.
   But no happen.
Think maybe they hide for surprise party so good they get lost or maybe die in

horrible get-suffocate-from-hide in-old-freezer accident. WORRY!!! But Bigfoot get wise to them. Know now friends just cheap, lazy, heartless no goods. Bigfoot decide do something nice for self for big day and sneak in they house at night and pick out own present and blow out flickering candle of life in they brains. Make a wish, jerks.

EMPIRE STATE

GIVE AND TAKE

Maybe you like a lot of people. Say
you used to like Bigfoot but feel
you have outgrown. "Moved on". Maybe
even hate Bigfoot. Think this book shitty.
  Well.
  Bigfoot think you shit too then. Have spent
  whole life trying give you quality entertain-
ment and never ask anything from you.
You leave out cookie and milk for
Santa and bear trap and rat poison for
Bigfoot. Listen, Bigfoot not trying
cry the blues and ask for
handouts, but really, would be
so hard for you to leave
out beer and porno just once
a year? Maybe every second year?
Leave by big tree in back yard please.

HAVE PROBLEM

Hello. This a little hard for me talk about. Guess everybody have deep dark secret so maybe should no feel ashame. Just come out and say it. Bigfoot addicted to eat garbage. Start out just recreational. Was at party with raccoons and they offer some. Eat and at first feel nothing, then

maybe little buzz, Pretty soon couldn't get enough. Wake up in morning and first thing do is eat garbage, No even matter what kind. Rich people garbage, poor people garbage. Walk around for a week with old mayonnaise jar stuck on hand and just not care. One day find self living at dump. Bigfoot clean for months now but still day to day, Please help by store you garbage in can with locking lid, or put something real heavy on top.

TRICKS

When times slow Bigfoot go to corner for earn some cash money.

Find humiliating but necessary.

PRICE LIST

Roll over $2.73

Sit $1.50
Sit/Stay $18.00

Shake
$3.00

GAS

Arson $14.00

GOOD TO GOODER

Bigfoot pretty amazing guy. Most mystifying thing about Bigfoot not really how evade society for so long, not what have hide in blood soak sack or how keep look so good when other forest creature look like shit. You ever wonder "what the fuck I taste secret ingredient in Bigfoot salad dressing?" NO TELL! Better question you should be ask Bigfoot is "Bigfoot, how you always stay on sunny side of life?"

Well, if want truth Bigfoot have bad days too. Not always feel like rainbow and sparkle inside. When feeling blue always find good belly laugh and beat something to death brighten day. Just pick weakest in pack, stalk mercilessly, catch and bash all me blues into they face. Think not so much helpless victim; rather,

Moist Towelette for The Soul.™

(Note: No eat thing after therapy kill, it now be full of evil spirit. Evil spirit taste like artificial watermelon.

Nobody likes this.

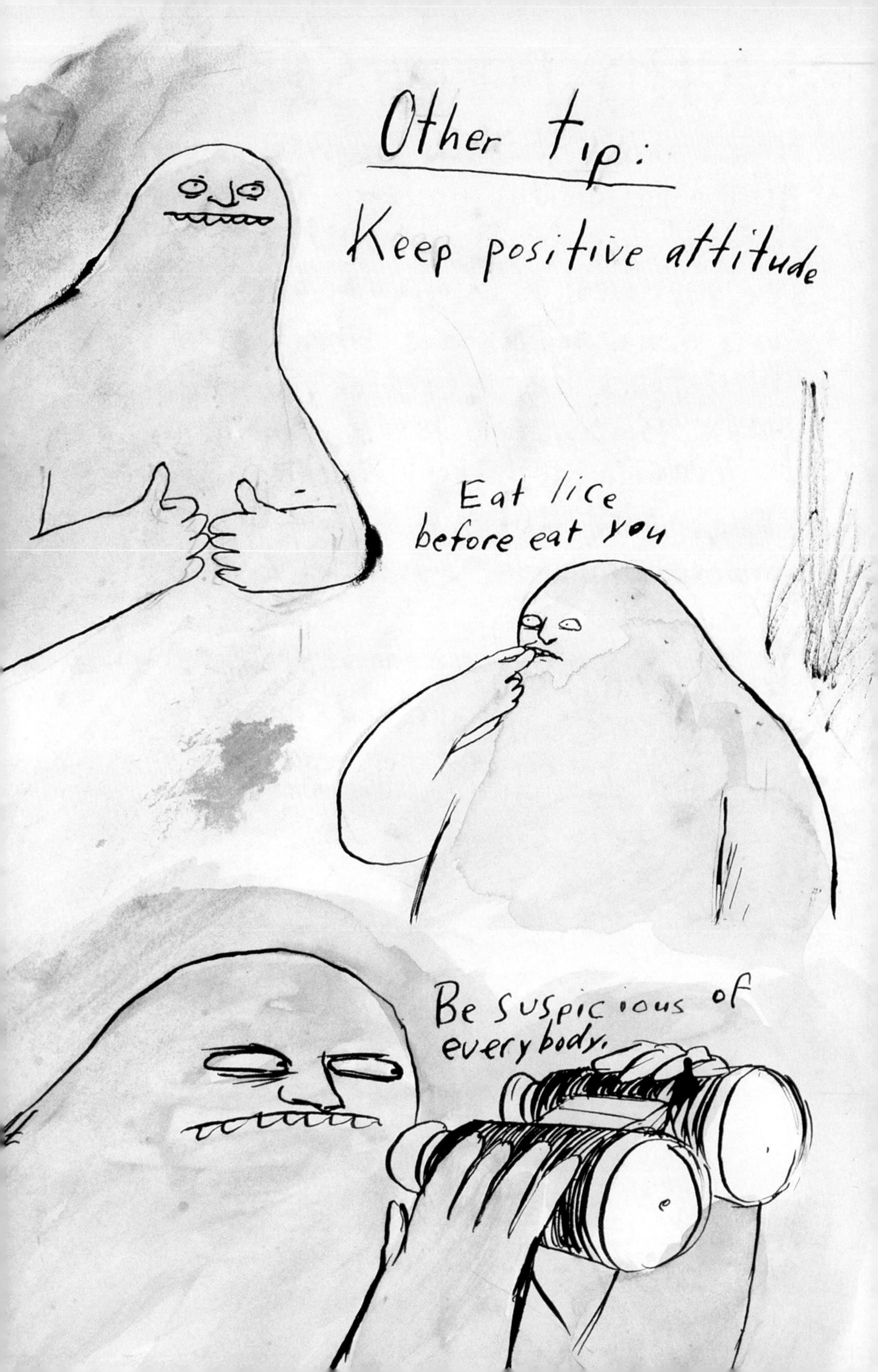

Other tip:

Keep positive attitude

Eat lice
before eat you

Be suspicious of
everybody.

WORD TO WISE

Have cocktails with very successful business tycoon. After many crantini he lean over and tell secret of him success. He say "never let them see you sweat.". Disappointing because Bigfoot cover in hair and no can tell when Bigfoot sweat unless touch Bigfoot (which generally should not do). Bigfoot real problem under pressure be involuntary snot bubble, trickle of vomit, surprise turd and mist of pee. Cry and earwax fountain too. Sweat not much of issue.

Bigfoot suppose advice can be apply to any body secretion, it just that "never let them see you earwax" not have same ring to it.

TOUGH CROWD

Laughter is almost best medicine.
Slightly less potent than antibacterial
distilled from Bigfoot cerebro-spinal
fluid.
Regardless, laughter also good and easier
harvest.
This why Bigfoot aspiring stand up comic.
Write own stuff.   It good.

   You Laugh.

- So I talking to a moose today and it
  get shot in head by hunter and hunter
  all like "You going to eat THAT?"
  and I say "No way, this guy was asshole
  and I not a big fan of JERKY!"

- So some chick walk in bar and say
   "Rabbi, Priest, Minister?" and I say
   "NO, I BIGFOOT!" Chicks, huh?

- What weird shape, full of things
  and good to eat?
      - OK, I eat!!!

BIGFOOT WILL

Bigfoot being of sound mind do hereby leave following instructions regarding final wishes and disbursement of me estate upon event of Bigfoot be dead.

---

① To executors of will, it Bigfoot wish that you have Bigfoot body cut into thirds and burned on funeral pyre in lobby of following institutions:
- Museum of Natural History
- People Magazine
- National Enquirer

Then tell them go screw self, they no never get Bigfoot

② Collect ashes and Bigfoot treasures and hide in secret tomb you build. Maybe a parade be good to have before so pique public interest about secret tomb. Secret tomb only cool if people know it exist somewhere and die trying to find.

Also spread rumor of magic curative mystic power of officially license Bigfoot Dear® Commemorative collector merchandiase.

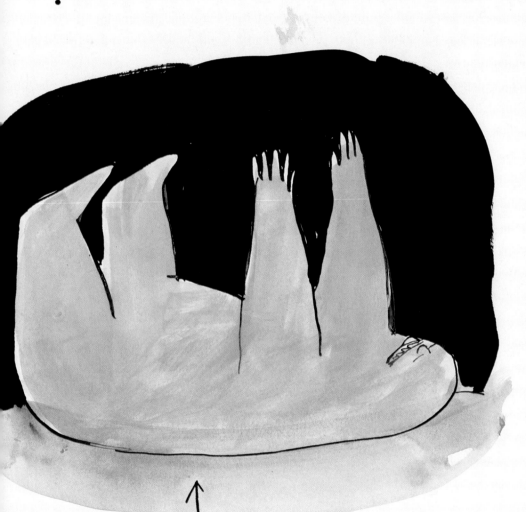

NOTE
Have be careful, sometime Bigfoot just play dead for avoid predator tresponsibility. Will not enforceable if just fake dead.

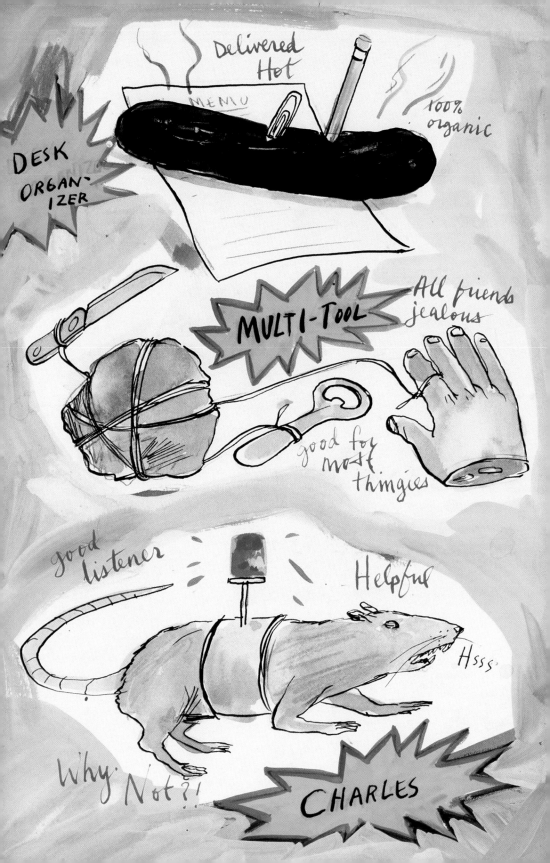